UNDER THE STEEL YOKE

*

POEMS

JABULANI MZINYATHI

Mwanaka Media and Publishing Pvt Ltd,
Chitungwiza Zimbabwe
Creativity, Wisdom and Beauty

Publisher:
Mmap

Mwanaka Media and Publishing Pvt Ltd

24 Svosve Road, Zengeza 1

Chitungwiza Zimbabwe

mwanaka@yahoo.com

https//mwanakamediaandpublishing.weebly.com

Distributed in and outside N. America by African Books
Collective

orders@africanbookscollective.com

www.africanbookscollective.com

ISBN: 978-0-7974-8491-7

EAN: 9780797484917

DISCLAIMER

ACKNOWLEDGEMENTS

I am eternally grateful to Tendai Rinos Mwanaka for
suggesting that I come up with this compilation and
basically working on it with me. I am deeply indebted
to Mbizo Chirasha of Miombo Publishing for being a
merciless critic who read these poems and made
useful suggestions. I am also grateful to my wife and
two children who never read these works but always
ask about whether royalties will flow like the mighty
Zambezi River! Like my compatriot Dambudzo
Marechera 'my name is not money but mind.' Last
but not least I am grateful to the Zimbolicious Poetry
family for the renewed hope in poetry.

Contents

Introduction by Tendai R. Mwanaka

In traditional African life cattle yokes were made from tree trunks, and these, when the ox was in a dire situation, like when the rope was strangling its neck, it could break the yoke to get out, or die from strangling. With these wooden yokes, there was an alternative, breaking the yoke but with a steel yoke, there seems to be no alternative... the ox can only accept its death, or carrying it until the end, maybe until the owner of this steel yoke decides to unyoke it. This is the feeling one might have with the title of Jabulani Mzinyathi's poetry book, *Under The Steel Yoke.*

Under The Steel Yoke is a collection of what I might term struggle or protest poems from the Zimbabwean poet, Jabulani Mzinyathi, whom I have had the liberty to work with, in several publications I have edited or published, among others, *Zimbolicious poetry anthology.* We arranged this book into 6 sections, each section covering an important part of struggle poetry.

In the first part, *Derailed Leadership*, we are instantly introduced to who this poet is in his other life. Jabulani Mzinyathi is a provincial magistrate in the courts of Zimbabwe. In this first poem he takes us into this other world of his, inside the courtroom. We see with the narrator the inner workings of the courtroom, but this courtroom is inside the poet who is wrestling with his mind, and his mind is accusing him of remaining silent in the face of persecution wrought on the innocent. It brings into form the Catholic conception of what a social sin is. When you have the ability to fight for the helpless and refuse to do so, the Catholics believes you commit a social sin. He follows the trial up to the last sentence, "how do you plead: guilty or not guilty." Guilty! Do you say, but the poet doesn't tell us how the narrator pleaded. This is the true hallmark of the storyteller in this poet. He leaves you hanging, trying to find solutions or interpretations.

And he hints on his solution a poem later, "divine intervention". It is a call he goes back to in several upcoming poems. Has the poet given up, waiting for the bigger voice, that of the divine. In this section he also delves into the 'exilitic' condition, which weighs even a lot harder on the narrator as he deals with the nonentity of his existence and nowhere else to go situation he is in. In another section, a little later he revisits this exile land again as he lists the issues that the persecuted faces in the land of exile. In the poem, *Those Ravings* you feel it is an open take-on at one of the most virulent politicians in Zimbabwe, Jonathan

Moyo, whom some many poems latter he also makes a vitriolic attack on in the poem *To A Nutty Professor*, which actually was the nickname we used on Moyo as he turned from being a well respected political analyst and fierce critic of the government of Robert Mugabe into his fiercest supporter around the turn of the century. The poet notes how this politician has used the podium to attack everyone who thinks otherwise. But in this poem the character could be Mugabe who hasn't shied away from using every podium to attack his detractors too. The poet here becomes a politician and grapples with the political situation in his amidst.

Mzinyathi uses well the Germany's dichten denken (poetry and thought) form on the poem, *Holding On*. "What relay race/When the baton is not passed/What competition is this? When there is one competitor." Here we see the combination of thought and poetry; it is a simple worded poem but speaks with weight. And he calls again for "divine intervention" you will be mistaken to think he is calling for the Christian gods but as you read the whole collection, this poet calls his own gods, gods of his culture, a god of struggle, a god of consciousness. He has no respect for the god the priests preach. He assigns the same anger to the priest that he assigns to the politician. He loops them together. They steal from the poor to enrich themselves. He also tackles youth gullibility, and tells the youths to refrain from being used by the corrupt politician to help them stay in power.

In the second part he deals with violence. The poem that strikes me is entitled, *Chill In My Spine.* Here the poet interweaves the facets of the dark worlds in trying to investigate the violence the politicians have meted on the mass. He piles image after image of the dark worlds. We see maggots, corpses, vultures, crows, vampires, hellish bats, eerie caves, ominous echoes, all these are "slogans of death". There is a beautiful, a dark kind of beautiful layering up of these facets of the dark worlds, one on top of the next to create a weave of suffering, soul numbing. You travel with the narrator in this dark world, you feel your breathe, the chills, as you hear these slogans of death. It leaves you beat, down, broken, dead. In the next poem he lists again the signs of a failed thing, the death of a state and ends with a call for divine intervention. The repetitiveness of the images, hammer-hitting you, relentlessly, there is no rest for the poet, why should there be rest for the reader, works well with this genre of protest poetry.

In the next poem he re-imagines this political violence and persecution and compares it to that of

Goebbels, the father of pain. We clearly see the Hitlerian ideology in the purported degree of violence that the government of Mugabe is known for, and the images pile on with petrol bombs being thrown on the innocent and the absence of the truth. He says the truth becomes an offence in this situation. But he refuses to call the truth a sin. It's only the truth that wills his redemption, later in the book.

This poet is a master at listing things, images. I felt it was like the way the reggae artists of yesteryear, Bob Marley, Peter Tosh, Barrington Levy etc created reggae music through the act of listing of images. I know the poet is a huge fan of the above artists. Each image builds on the next one or works totally alone. The poet becomes the prophet. He leads the readers to the window and leaves the readers standing by the window. Its upto the reader to open the curtain and see beyond the window to find their body. The readers have to fashion out their body from these lists of images. In the poem, *Bereaved*, he mourns the country that Zimbabwe has become- dead, and the last line harks back to the bible's- Ecclesiastes, which is the book of wisdom. Zimbabwe needs wisdom to raise itself from the dead postures that it is in.

In part 3 he focuses on resilience, fighting on, never giving up. The poet encourages the mass to continue with the struggle, to be defiant in struggle, to find moral regeneration. The poem *Dreams*, captures what the poet wants to achieve with this section of poems, to shorn light on the darkness, not really that, rather to use darkness to light darkness. It is the state of dreams bereft, that begins the healing process, and the healing miracle resides in this state. We need to use our dark bottoms to raise, to rise up. I like the way he kept repeating the word dreams, in dreams contained, stomped, deferred... to create rhyme, rhythm and energy in the poem. Dreams becomes the leitmotiv to move the poem, to move us, and ultimately to move the mass to find healing and hope.

In part 4 he explores the artist in the poet, who resurfaces plainly into sight. We see the work of the artist, that of the "society's conscience". He exhorts the artists to not be afraid of persecution, to tell the truth, which some poems before he had refused to call sin. In part 5 we see the reclamation of good ideals from the tragedies of the past. The poem *Thoughts* is striking in this section in that the poet even questions his own voice, his authority, that of the "discordant voice". Maybe he is trying to figure if it is good enough in itself to reclaim the good ideals. In the last section he deals with hope. He says the poet still hopes, the mass still hopes. In the last poem *Certainty*, he makes us realise that just like, "The sun will set/ Dawn will sprout/ Birds will twitter/ The cocks will crow/ Each one to their chores/ That is how it is/ That is how it should be/ The children will play/ On the road to the future."

Hope is always a certainty!

v v

UNDER THE STEEL YOKE

The wiry and ghoulish
The hand of despondency
This unfortunate present
Tightly in its steel fingers grip
The warped ideas
Chaining the present and the future
Crest fallen, led by stale ideas
Pummelled by vicious propaganda
Self- proclaimed saviours
Shamelessly clipping our wings
Desirous of making us automatons

CLEANSING

And what has been hidden
From the wise and the prudent
To the babe and the suckling
It shall be revealed
From off the wall the plaster falls
That selflessness of old
 The seamless revolutionary love
The youths should know
Posterity should hold firmly
For the health of this nation

THE CHARGES

You are brought before this court
You are charged with serious offences
Multiple counts of not speaking
Not speaking for the voiceless
Condoning and perpetuating brutality
Not speaking against their profligacy
Not speaking against acrid propaganda
Thus perpetuating nauseating lies
Not speaking against glorified violence
Violence spread for political gain
You are brought before this court
For you are a co-principal offender
Your silence was tantamount to acquiescence
Your inaction aided and abetted misrule
You turned a blind eye to the sufferers
You chose to be indifferent
You did not extinguish the run- away fire
You sang songs of praise in place of dirges
How do you plead? Guilty or not guilty?

THIS TIME

What fiery inferno is this
Devouring this nation
What is this sadistic brute
Holding us by the throat
Strangling this once beautiful nation
These are the wayward children
Now like leopards mauling parents
These directionless bastards
Sucked into the vortex of violence
These messengers of death
The tentacles of fear spread
Everywhere vibrations of violence
In the floods of terror we drown
Softly fall showers of tolerance
See the parched throat of this nation
The time for divine intervention is nigh

IN EXILE

The reverberations of the song
Still there in your befuddled mind
The streets of foreign lands roaming
You who walked tall and proud
Now you carry the burden of repression
That sparkle is long gone, gone, gone
That lacklustre weather-beaten suit
A size too small it now has become
That charisma is gone, gone, gone
Hallucinations are now your daily bread
You lie now in the trash can of history
The caustic fruits of villainy you chose
On you the sycophants heap all the blame
The reverberations of those dirges
Haunt you even beyond your watery grave

THOSE RAVINGS

They take to podiums
They slander
They ridicule
To shame bringing
Men of integrity
Belittling them
The ululations hear
 Deafening empty ululations

To podiums they take
Their demonic ways displayed
Shameless spin doctors
Taking advantage of the gullible
They shit and piss on those faces
See the rampant abuse
Those men of little minds

They take to podiums
The gospel of hate spreading
Noble ideals trivialising
To the wise mocking themselves
In their shameless efforts to mock others
Frothing at their loud mouths
To scorn exposing themselves

They impotently take to podiums

Their barrenness exposing
Their vanity pedestal placing
Exposing their desperation
Their words shall not take root
In the minds of the discerning
Men of honour shall be saluted
Though to vitriolic attacks subjected
Time shall be the judge

HOLDING ON

What relay race
When the baton is not passed
What competition is this
When there is one competitor

THE CURSED ONES

This explosion
This implosion
The maggots shall not have it
Here where it belongs
Trouble their consciences
The consciences they trample
Those that have personalised
Personalised our struggle
Those self- righteous bigots
Raping this throttled nation
We shall remember them

POLITICIANS AND PRIESTS

The dominance submerges discussion
That elevation to the podium
The raping of the mesmerised audience
Those that submit to your barren talk
Listening to your befuddling poly tricks
Listening to your self-glorification
Politicians and priests in the same mould
Thriving best where fear spreads
But listen now to this ant voice
That ominous warning: Beware the Ides of March
That myth of your invincibility shattered
King Owl's horns exposed for what they were
That folk tale still holds that lesson

PRIORITIES

Thrown in is the virility
Of the mass of unemployed youths
Bolstering waning popularity
Of the false kings of the earth

Bereft of nation building ideas
Skeletons in their cupboards
Now they have run short of cupboards
Tumbling out now are the skeletons

Holding tight to illusions
With cheap t-shirts and intoxicants
Youths remorselessly snuffing out lives
Trying vainly to keep the inevitable at bay

Part 2: WAVES OF DESPAIR

IN THE DUNGEONS

Aftermaths of the orgy
Orgy of deranging violence
Succumbing to their schemes
Lessons learnt from Old Nick
Bereft of any traces of humanity
Lynching those that think differently
Manacled by the demons
Minds submerged in hallucinations
Alone in the psychiatric ward
Languishing beyond redemption
Echoes of the extirpation of lives
Tossing in the whirlpool of derangement
Ghostly laughing where no joke is cracked
It pricks not their consciences
Youthful minds in a thick mist
Refuse now to be an automaton

CHILL IN MY SPINE

Ominous darkness
Flashes of lightning
Maggots in the corpse
Vulture beaks tearing
The competing crows everywhere
The shrieking vampires
Hellish bats in eerie caves
The ominous echoes
Slogans of death
A chill through my spine

BITTERNESS IN MY MOUTH

Scatter brained bastards
Despicable scoundrels, miscreants
To constrict thoughts
Their heinous mission
Societal light snuffing out
Civilisation fast sinking
Intolerance like a bird of prey soars
Despondency, despondency
Its ugly head rearing
The deadly scythe of violence
Under siege, under siege
In the stranglehold of tentacles
Engulfed in thick smoke
Bludgeoned by intolerance
A nation on the brink of death
Divine intervention now

THESE CRACKS

Yarn after yarn is spun
The Goebbels like doctors
Hammering us relentlessly
Vicious tall tales
Political party thugs
Amassing degrees in violence
Capped in the morgues
Fireworks displays
The flaming petrol bombs
Conspicuous by its absence
Is the painful truth
The excruciating pain of today
The succulent fruit of tomorrow
The truth is an offence
It shall never be a sin

MARECHERA VINDICATED

Now you are vindicated
The hunger and the drought
Thought that chapter was closed
The sting in those words
That play – the toilet
Nothing to queue for
This barrenness all around
Poverty holds us by our throats
Shelves full of toilet paper
Very few defecate any more
Dambudzo- the prophetic voice

KILLING SEASON

Thugs at the helm
Spattered brains
Deaths at door steps
The sadism everywhere
Murder in the air
Rising waves of brutality
Deserted homes
Licked by tongues of fire
Those wailing souls
In the steel grip of evil
Evil seemingly triumphant
Killers on the loose
Fatal scythes everywhere

STENCH OF ARROGANCE

Hear the wailing
Anguish in the ghettoes

The stench of failure
The putrid arrogance

The avoidable deaths
Graves gobbling many

Hairy maggots in morgues
Life rendered worthless

Rivers of raw sewage
Many a life drowned

Hear the wailing
The wailing in the ghettoes

BEREAVED

Once respected, hero worshipped
Now reviled and rejected
Once vibrant and vivacious
In sickly slumber wallowing
The scum of the earth
In a dance of death

Once great among nations
Now become a widow
Once the bread basket
Now a perennial beggar
Singing pitiful songs for survival

Minds in the grip of terror
The patriots turned traitors
Hens feeding on their own eggs
Visitors refusing to go
Making all sorts of weird excuses
The timelessness of Ecclesiastes

VICTIMS

Driven by dreams of Egoli
That place of elusive gold
That place of the elusive rand
Driven from the burning home
Evading the murderous gangs
Evading those man eating crocodiles
Scavenging for an existence
Still chasing after those illusions
Jumping from the frying pan into the fire
The shacks razed to the ground
The gruesome deaths in the slums
The victims of the victims
The real foe remains unscathed
Like amoeba poverty multiplies

[Egoli – place of gold. Name by which Johannesburg
is usually referred to]

COUNTERFEIT HISTORY

Jackboot kicks
Self-preservation poly tricks
Disused mine shafts
The true story cannot be concealed
Soon we shall know
The other side of the coin
Defiled are the roots of this struggle
The children starve
The children are thirsty
You shit and piss in the wells
The granaries of truth you burn
The truth is an offence but not a sin
I stand accused now
But see the tables shall be turned
The path of truth is laden with thistles and thorns
Limitless resilience we long espoused

THE EXECUTIONER QUESTIONED

Tell me now of how you sleep
In tranquillity do you sleep?
Succulent dreams do you ever have
At peace with your creator
By cold sweat not startled
With blood congealing screams
Piercing your ear drums
Tell me how do you sleep
Wailing widows in the background
Widowers assailed by agony
Hear heart rending wails of orphans
All those yearning for revenge
Itching to now hang you
The noose around your shrivelled balls
Just tell me how you sleep
As you continually smite your conscience
Perhaps you never had one
All those murders and celebrations
Your shrewd manipulation exhibited
Cheered on by your pawns
Tell me now: How do you sleep

DREAMS

Bereft of dreams
Dreams bashed by truncheons
Dreams under the jackboots
The jackboots of philistines
Dreams in solitary confinement
Dreams whimpering for freedom
That is the healing of this nation

THE EXORCISM

See the dark clouds
The dark clouds of evil

The air is humid
Fanged hate speech

What now nation builders
All the mud slinging

Listen to the statesmen
Their words pure venom

Frothing at their mouths
No distinction between opponents and foes

To the throne by any means
Murder, rape, kidnapping

The nation lifeless
In the web of fear

See the dark clouds
The dark clouds of evil

The thunder of their oratory
The lightning of poverty

Satisfying their evil egos
Nothing for us in all this

We refuse to be cannon fodder
Refuse to be pawns in their games

THE RAPED FUTURE

I am the raped future
Look at me and you will understand
See the deep physical wounds
Inflicted on me by political thugs
The psychological scars of propaganda
The past and present raped me
I am the raped future
Now standing at street corners
Facing choking unemployment levels
Waylaying travellers by road sides
Driven by need and not greed
Selling pounds of flesh in bars and brothels
Languishing in putrid prison cells
I am the battered and bruised future
Eking a living on South African farms
Vainly evading violent arrests and detentions
Waiting and waiting for deportation at Lindela
Back home to face naked brutality
Hoping that one day the sun will shine again

[Lindela is a prison in South Africa where illegal
immigrants are held pending deportation]

TIME NOW

Time now for moral regeneration
To salvage those ideals
To do serious introspection
Collective conscience trampled for too long
Time to clean up the mess
To wipe away the stench of greed

Time now for moral regeneration
Rapists, killers, pimps and prostitutes
Driven into the crevices of society
Never again to be pedestal placed
Listen to this wailing nation
Time now for moral regeneration

SHOOTING STRAIGHT

What is this patriotism they talk of
Another of their poly tricks
Asking us to go to shells of hospitals
Asking us to go to remains of schools
Off they go to western capitals
And now to the eastern capitals
Getting the treatment they deny us
Dying in droves of avoidable diseases
Getting the education they deny us
Nurturing the ignorance that is our demise
Now show me the true patriots
These visitors have overstayed their welcome

TIME COMES

With all its dexterity
Off the branches
The monkey will fall

The deep sea diver
With that proficiency
Shall in a pond drown

The noose tightens
Around the hang man's neck
Now the tables have been turned

IN THE CORRIDORS

Waging a vicious war
A protracted war
Against imagined foes

Clutching at a straw
Drowning man's futile exercise
For the end is at hand

Trying to hold back the time
Failure on the pedestal
That is a sore fact

In procrastination
There's no permanence
The inevitable is nigh

The time is not far

NOT HEEDED

And when the artist speaks
Through deft brush strokes
On canvas, on paper...
Through the chipping chisel
On the marble, soapstone
Through the songs about all the wrongs
Through the prancing lines
The prancing lines of bitter sweet poetry
That soothsayer I hear
That court jester now warning
Let those that have ears hear

BEAST OF BURDEN

The artist
A beast of burden
Society's ills
To the fore bringing
Society's conscience
The search for the truth
At times censored
Persecuted, reviled
Jailed, tortured, murdered
'The truth is an offence'
Exposing the hypocrisy
Devils quoting the scriptures
The indefatigable artist
A beast of the nation's burden
Poet, painter, sculptor, singer…
Persecution is your coronation

MORSEL SNATCHED

At the apex of salivating
The morsel snatched
Sadistic brutes at work
Paranoid at the prospects of success
Under the steel yoke of warped ideas
Propagating diabolic perceptions
Shredded by the censors' scissors
Blossom then undaunted spirit
This fire cannot be extinguished
Ideas held captive seek liberation
Sprout then O shoot of resilience
Shout triumphantly O muffled voice

TO A NUTTY PROFESSOR

Then you had incisive thoughts
Delivering telling blows you did
The thunder and lightning of protest
Then you tasted their evil candy
Joined the obscene wining and dining
The songs of praise submerged the dirges
Will you say you were like cancer
Din of doubt in our expectant minds
The protracted assault on independent minds
Those draconian, muzzling pieces of legislation
That we will forever bitterly remember

TRIUMPH

The dropping bombs
Bombs of propaganda
Bombarding my brain paths

All these gods
Seeking to cage my mind
Weaving their webs

Torrents of religions
Seeking to drown my soul
The din of futility

The vibrancy of my roots
Repelling these schemes
The din of triumph

Part 5: IDEALS RECLAIMED

HEALING THE NATION

Warped are the ideals
Suiting the opportunists
The barrenness abounds
A frigid and putrid history
To posterity revolting
Spin doctors' manipulation repelled
That is the consciousness
Transforming slaves into real men
Shaping our derailed destiny
Kicking official history in the face
That selflessness of old
That revolutionary love
The youths should know
Posterity should hold firmly
For the health of this nation

CAUTION

What warped nationalism is this?
What warped pan Africanism is this
Pretending to fight this imperialism
By night selling the sacred inheritance
Betraying those bones not yet interred
Betraying that blood not yet dry
Keeping fellow citizens in chains
The chains of fear and poverty
Handing over trinkets to praise singers
And the ever present opportunists
I reject this blind pan Africanism
Clapping and ululating to aid violence
Aiding black on black violence, yes
To spite the enslavers, colonisers, imperialists
See they hide behind revolutionary rhetoric
Their deception is destined for the dung heap

NEVER AGAIN

Never again shall we be subjected
Subjected to the profanation of the sacrosanct
The sacrosanct symbols of our struggle
Never again should there be arrogance
The arrogance of self-proclaimed saviours
Leaving people to burn in the blazing sun
While in hotels they fill their insatiable bellies
With hounds and concubines forever in tow
Inflammatory speeches should forever be gone
Statesmen and women should take to podiums
Messages of nation building should resonate
The time for the healing of this nation is nigh

TRUTH AND RECONCILIATION

Down memory lane
Through all that pain
For healing this nation
That is the challenge
For truth and reconciliation
Those hideous secrets reveal
Those shallow graves
The disused mine shafts
For the healing of the perpetrator
For healing the battered survivor
For the souls of the victims
This story must be told
The future demands appeasement

LESSONS FOR THE FUTURE

When what has been hidden
From the wise and the prudent
Has to the babe and the suckling been revealed
When that cup of evil is to brim full
When those stories of old are told
When the seditious songs are sung
That is when this biting winter is gone
That shall be the healing of this nation
That fear of truth shall be gone
When the unrepentant shall repent
That shall be the healing of this nation
That is when the lessons for the future are drawn
Drawn from the tragedies of the past

THOUGHTS

Thought we were in it together
Thought we were our own liberators
Thought you were by altruism driven
Did not know of latent mercenary tendencies
Thought the birds would freely twitter
Thought there would be a relay race
Thought of the market place of ideas

Did not know this would be a discordant voice

Thought there would be abundance of bliss
Thought that the laws would achieve justice
Thought there would be no stinking opulence
Did not know that I was wide off the mark

FREEDOM SONG

I yearn for lots of space
Lots of room for me to grow
Don't want to be a potted plant
With my branches trimmed
By the merciless gardeners
I yearn for lots of space
Being closeted brings trepidation
Don't want to be a caged bird
Want to soar through the air
To perch on the mountain peaks
I detest this stifling domestication
I am a dove not a pigeon
I will never be a Brahman bull
Watch out I am a goring buffalo

PROPHECY

It shall be so O children
When the right time comes
The prophets still speak today
Through the brush strokes on the canvas
Through the incisive chisels
Through all those musical instruments
The prophets still speak today
Through the prancing prose, poetry and song
Those that do not understand today
They shall wallow in mental squalor
Those that do not understand today
Shall tomorrow in deep regret sink
Listen to the prophets in timelessness
The prophets in the garden of inspiration
Listen to that divine inspiration
Listen to this divine inspiration
Forever listen to the prophets

Part 6: HOPING STILL

UNDER SIEGE

Sowing despondency
The hyacinth of despair

See the whimpering nation
This nation under siege

See the lightning
Hear the thunder

Gullibility wreaking havoc
Fun time for thugs

Freeing us to enslave us
Contradictions in the hijacked struggle

Remorselessly using the bullet
To influence the ballot

After the storm calm shall return

FROM DUSK TO DAWN

Those guns
Shall spit fire at the real enemies

Those truncheons
Flesh they shall rip off
Off the backs of the people's foes

That biting tear smoke
In the right direction shall drift

By the sword they shall die
For by the sword they live

Listen children
The prophets have spoken

Songs of redemption
Songs of triumph
Listen!

THIS WINTER

This winter
Its approach I long saw
Now the bared fangs of chilly gusts
These sore sights of desolation
This thick wintry darkness
Those exuberant spirits
In the embrace of numbness
In the claws of bleakness
This winter shall be gone

TWICE RAPED

The indelible scars
After the heinous crime
Raped first by a foreign bandit
Next raped by kith and kin
The trauma shall subside
That time is not far

HOME SWEET HOME

Emaciated shadows
This barrenness

This dry season
Cacti everywhere

Rustling dry leaves
This whirlwind

Broken dreams
Fractured lives

Torrents of despair
Harbinger of hope

VICTORY

The clouds part
Sunshine filters through
Blades of grass everywhere
The sun shines
Dew takes fight
Songs of victory in the air

VENCEREMOS

In cheap t-shirts clad
Fed on alcohol and drugs
Spreading the web of fear
Propping the ominous personality cult
Messengers of death everywhere
Kith and kin bludgeoning to death
One song must be sung
Waves of intolerance spreading
Chaining those desirous of freedom
Out of this morass, our lives
Bursting out of this bud of poverty
Between the hammer and tongs of hardships
Fashioning real men and women

[*Venceremos* is a Spanish word meaning we shall
overcome]

THE NEW SONG

This has been a long night
This thick wintry darkness
The sad song of croaking frogs
The rumbling of thunder, lightning flashing
The eerie hooting of owls
Hyenas laughing in the distance

This has been a long walk
The way thistle and thorn laden
Stumbling, falling and rising again
At the back of the mind the refrain
The darkest hour is before dawn

The first rays of the rising sun
The sweet songs of birds
The doves cooing in the distance
The cymbals of African laughter
The vivacity of life plain to see

CERTAINTY

The sun will set
Dawn will sprout
Birds will twitter
The cocks will crow
Each one to their chores
That is how it is
That is how it should be
The children will play
On the road to the future

Printed in the United States
By Bookmasters